How To Get Your Crush to love you

Good, Fast, Easy Ways To Help You Get Your Crush

By

Jennet Joel

Table of Contents

Introduction

Liking somebody is something typical.

Getting to know someone else and making them like you requires a ton of exertion. You can't drive somebody to cherish you. Love is something enchanted. Be that as it may, there are ways you can expand the possibilities your crush will, at last, cherish you.

Chapter One
Speaking With Your Crush

Initiate a discussion. Talking is an extremely viable method for getting to know someone and checking whether they share similar interests as you do. Beginning a discussion or simply a fast visit will likewise assist you with knowing regardless of whether they are into you. Simply don't push it. Keep it fascinating.

Converse with them routinely making casual chitchat, and once in a while discuss more serious things or take part in an extensive discussion. Assuming that the discussion normally develops and you begin to share insider facts or dreams, you will bond. Listen to a ton, and answer humanely. Try not to make the discussion about you.

Perhaps you ought to go belly up. Think about it, at any rate, when all is good and well. Let your crush know how you feel. Let it all out without a moment's delay. Simply ensure both of you are separated from everyone else and that you express it as nonchalantly as possible.

Attempt to be in similar gatherings if you go to a similar school. Continuously grin at your crush however not excessively anxiously. Do it barely enough to inspire them to grin back and stroll over to you. Request their Snapchat, Instagram, or Facebook because it's more subtle than requesting a telephone number, yet you'll have the subtleties.

Convey your crush's coquettish messages, and check whether they answer. Attempt to convey messages verbally and through non-verbal communication. These signs of interest will tell your crush (intentionally or subliminally) that you are smashing on them, and they may very well fall in love with you.

Give little clues with your non-verbal communication. This might occur all alone. Watch for signs that your crush is doing this as well. Open up to your crush, and go ahead and show the individual your weak side. You want to tell your crush (silently) that they are extraordinary.

Snicker a great deal. Get a little coy. Say the individual's name. Individuals love hearing their names being said. Praise the individual. Remember to be caring and magnificent.

Contact your crush in a coquettish manner, not in an unpleasant way. Contact the individual's arm. It will show that you like them, however, it won't make them think you need to date them on the off chance that they would rather not. Just softly contact their shoulder, give them a high-five, or even an embrace farewell. Chomp your lip, hesitantly grin when they bother you, run your fingers through your hair, and squint more than expected.

Visually connect. These things simply occur. Getting somebody to see you is hard, as is keeping their consideration. Assuming that you believe somebody should see you, visually engage, yet not for a long time. It's similar to playing with a little pet and hanging a string right in front of them. Pulling the string this way keeps paying attention.

This doesn't mean you gaze at your crush continually. That can give anybody a major jerk factor. To visually engage with your crush, you ought to look at them, grin, and afterward put your head down or turn away timidly. This will give them a clue that you like them without cracking them out.[6]

Eye-to-eye connection likewise conveys certainty, which is interesting to the vast majority since it's an approach to building closeness. Enamored individuals have more eye-to-eye connections.

Over our 20+ years in the relationship business, a huge number of individuals have tracked down affection in harmony...could you be straightaway? Check us out when you're prepared for something genuine.

Chapter two
Interfacing with Your Crush

Make a fellowship, and be around your crush more. It is extremely normal for two companions/closest companions to experience passionate feelings for or extravagant each other after being companions for a seriously prolonged period. Understanding what your crush's leisure activities, interests, and mood killers are will help your possibilities turn into their partner.[8]

Have a go at conversing with them as a companion first. If you approach the individual as a pound, they will just see you as somebody who likes them. This might be hazardous if they could do without you since they will be more averse to the need to get to know you. Become companions first, and afterward attempt to seek after them.

Ensure they feel good around you, through correspondence. Get to know them and told them you (what you like, what you don't like....etc.) This decides if you are viable or not.

Invest more energy with the individual. Spend time with them. Not one-on-one yet, yet perhaps ask your crush and a couple of different companions to go to the recreation area or approach play computer games or something to that effect. Along these lines, you can see and connect in a more regular environment.[9]
Do exercises together. The more you cooperate, the more they'll think about you. It's an easy decision!
In the end, you could inquire as to whether they needed to accomplish something easygoing with you one-on-one. Perhaps it's a game or a film. Sort out what intrigues them and straightforwardness into the idea.

Try not to drive it excessively far excessively quickly. Aside from having a despondent or constrained relationship, pushing things too quick could likewise demolish the bond you've previously made, which could prompt losing them as a companion too. Show restraint!
Sticking is something individuals detest most seeing someone. Give your crush their space, and let any relationship unfurl at a characteristic speed.

Try not to follow the individual. In addition to the fact that this is unseemly, it tends to be unlawful - and it doesn't work. Try not to play wildly with the smash. Try not to ensure you hear everything about this individual, by the same token. Try not to attempt to continually associate with them. Assuming they could do like you, this will put them off.

Hang out together, have a good time, and talk. On the off chance that it's intended to be, it'll occur. If not, there are a lot of other fish in the ocean. Try not to attempt to make your crush love you. Love is certainly not a game.

Be an individual they can rely upon. They say the best connections comprise the best of companions! Get to know your crush, and they'll get to know you. All the more significantly, let them in on they can trust you and go to you.

Help the individual out at whatever point your crush needs assistance or support and show up for the pulverize brilliantly. Be mindful of their needs and needs. If your crush neglects lunch one day and you can bear to get them a tidbit or offer your lunch, they'll extraordinarily see the value in your benevolence and empathy.

Focus on them, and be there when they need it. Be the sort of individual they can depend on because you do what you say you will do. Be certifiable. Help your crush have a positive outlook on themself.

Get familiar with their inclinations. Get keen on things they are keen on. Say, for example, your crush loves everything about sports. Observe a few additional sporting events so that on the off chance that they begin discussing sports with your companions, you'll understand what they're talking about.[10]

If more established music, ask what their main tune is. Then, pay attention to the music, and check whether you can find comparative melodies they could likewise like.

Nothing remains at this point but to act naturally around your crush, and perceive how the cards work out. Make sure to focus on your crush's preferences and to know about their sentiments and their inclinations, however, don't take on interests that u.

Chapter three
Chipping away at Yourself

Put your best self forward yet, above all, be your regular self. Be straightforward with yourself and think: How perfect and self-caring would you say you are? Do you deal with your body? Try not to be pompous and narcissistic, yet make an honest effort to look great.

Have a feeling of style. You don't need to be a first-class fashionista, yet staying up with the latest and out-of-control will undoubtedly assist with getting your crush's attention. Looking new never harmed anyone. Perhaps pick one day seven days to spruce up a tad, yet make it ordinary and not excessively constrained

Look good and agreeable. Assuming that you wear a messy, messy dress, your crush probably shouldn't converse with you. If few new things for your closet, ensure they are your style. Sort out what matches your character and accents your best focuses.

Ensure that you smell lovely and are spotless. You should have a go at wearing a light scent. Have an unmistakable fragrance. Wear aroma/cologne, put on antiperspirant, clean your teeth and bite gum.

Grin a great deal, and keep an uplifting outlook. Individuals need to be with individuals who appear to be content and tomfoolery, not crotchety and negative. Your demeanor can go far.

The individual you have your eye on is bound to be thoughtful if you have an open stance, grin, and welcome them energetically, either by waving or grinning wickedly. Act glad to see somebody, however not so cheerful they imagine that you're following them. Creatures do this to people constantly. They act glad to see you, and individuals become glad to see them. Individuals even anticipate seeing them. It works.

Attempt to be pleasant to everybody and don't tear down others. What goes around, comes around. They will see the way you treat others. Self-image and haughtiness are rarely engaging. Be related to positive things.

Be sure about yourself. Try not to change what your identity is or rationalize it. Game playing and individuals who shape-shift to become

somebody they aren't will switch individuals off. Individuals like a touch of secret, and they are attracted to sure individuals.
Have a daily existence beyond them. The more you do, the more intriguing you become. Remember to likewise look cool yet fascinating. The seriously fascinating you become, the more captivated your crush will become about you.
Whether it's your body shape or your clever rebounds, you have a major area of strength for a. Sort it out, and when you do, resolve on bringing it.
Assuming that you need to change yourself to get your crush to like you, they're presumably not worth the effort. Most smashes don't endure over four months, and somebody better could go along. If your crush doesn't go off the deep end.

Understand that there are various types of squashes. The term 'squash' gets tossed around a ton. It can imply that you sing a fixation on somebody, or that you like them.
The Cordial/Non-romantic Smash (some of the time called a "crush"): It is critical to recollect that not all overwhelming inclinations are heartfelt, some of them can be dispassionate

too. Allowing yourself to trust somebody and become near somebody, without fundamentally having heartfelt affections for them, is a truly extraordinary thing. Needing to be around an individual all the time may simply imply that you have gone from companions to closest companions. It's generally expected to have a companion squash - you ought to need to spend time with your BFF however much as could be expected and have a non-romantic relationship with them.

Chapter four
The Deference Pound

When you venerate an individual (like a big name, educator, or cohort who has accomplished something cool) you might understand that you have extraordinary sentiments about that individual and what they have done. These sentiments may be confused with heartfelt sentiments essentially because they are so extreme. Feeling marginally awed by the sight of somebody who has accomplished something astounding or can show you incredible things is regular. Frequently, it's ideal to let a touch of time elapse before truly really mulling over these sentiments. By and large, whenever you have invested a ton of energy with this individual, you will have gained some significant experience from them and may start to feel like you can remain on the equivalent ground. You might find that your crush-like sentiments calm down once the underlying amazement of being in their presence wears off.

The Passing Smash: It is human instinct to be drawn to others. Regardless of whether you are

in an extraordinary relationship, you actually could find that you feel drawn to somebody other than your better half. This fascination is the very thing we call a passing to pulverize - this new individual might appear to be previously unheard-of, and they likely are, but that doesn't mean you ought to reexamine the relationship you are in or on the other hand, assuming you're single, drop all that to attempt to accompany them. Intermittently, passing squashes are spiked by being drawn in - most frequently actually - to somebody.
The Heartfelt Smash: Some of the time having eyes only for somebody implies you like them- - and in a heartfelt manner at that. Having a heartfelt pound implies that you need to accompany that individual in something other than a cordial way- - you need to be their significant about kissing, clasping hands with, or nestling with that individual, you presumably have a heartfelt smash.

How would you make your person impossible to make somebody love you in a flash? For one's purposes, you have zero control over how somebody feels. What's more, it requires investment for individuals to foster serious sensations of fondness like this. Simply unwind and take as much time as necessary. If it's intended to be, it will work out!

Question

How would I win the core of my crush?

Chapter five
Dance

If you are at a club or something and don't have the foggiest idea about this individual well overall, this is an extraordinary move. You can grab their eye by moving before him or them. If you are as of now dating this individual or have a heartfelt interest going and are someplace in private, you could do a hot striptease. Look at Carmen Electra's stuff for more!

I realize I've taken in her moves as a component of my exercise and its extraordinary activity. Additionally, you get to realize a wide range of provocative dance moves that you can use to make somebody fall hard for you! To get a fellow or young lady's consideration, knowing how to move well can get the job done because they will not have the option to turn away!

I've grabbed the eye of many folks through my dance moves. They see this large number of young ladies on the dance floor, however, I've learned procedures to move that make me stick out. For the most part, I have recently watched a ton of dance recordings which is where I realize what dance moves to break out when I hit the clubs or bars. Jam with the jukebox assuming you want to!

Send that person a message via web-based entertainment

To talk or can't talk for reasons unknown, you could continuously move toward them via online entertainment. Bounce onto Facebook and convey a companion demand; send an unknown GIF or emoticon across the web. Assuming you maintain that the person in question should see you, make certain to leave remarks on their web-based entertainment stages.

You have such countless choices here! You can like or cherish their stuff, send that person a puzzling, provocative message, or simply jab them in some way or another as a mysterious admirer. Get innovative when you attempt to contact that person along these lines! You'll in all actuality do fine and dandy acting naturally.

Chapter six
Put on a show

As indicated by Science every day playing past difficult to-get normal will work. You don't need to carry on like somebody you're not or make statements you wouldn't regularly say, yet you don't need to say all that strikes a chord all things considered. You need to leave a few things as a secret - something your crush should get a good grip on.

Be lively and coy with everybody to pull this off. As a reference, you would rather not be somebody you're not. If an extremely friendly individual strategy wouldn't be the right one for you, however, you could make it happen to assume that you as of now have an exceptionally friendly character. Simply carry on such as yourself, and you'd pull it off easily.

It would turn out perfect for you; simply make sure to watch out for the one you have eyes only for. You maintain that they should realize you are keen on them the most. You could visually connect a lot and grin a ton to show this, as well. You should spruce up a piece to show that you put some work into your hopes to get their eye.

The message that person a lot of messages Perhaps you two are now companions, and you need to have something other than a fellowship. If you can message each other, you could utilize a wide range of strategies to get their eye. Simply act naturally and express the way that you feel as such. Ensure that your message isn't excessively scandalous or questionable assuming you are uncertain about the response.

For instance, you should be careful while saying that you love the person in question on the off chance that you haven't been playing with each other for an extremely lengthy. This is because you would rather not seem to be serious areas of strength in text informing. Assuming you put yourself out there something over the top, you in all actuality do take a chance with dismissal, so be prepared to forget about that assuming it ends up like that.

Recollect that an educator or companion could peruse your message, so if it's for their eyes just, you might need to hold on until you are where you can talk so you can let them know face to face how you feel. Along these lines, you will not have meandering eyes perusing what you composed when it's not their concern. Couldn't you concur?

Conclusion

Relationship anticipate

Everything you can do is put yourself out there. Try to get to know them, invest energy with them, and be simply the most ideal adaptation that you can be. Try not to make a special effort to attempt to dazzle them or anything either, simply act naturally!

Tips

Bother them a piece, simply don't go too far!

Become more friendly. Gradually become increasingly more OK with your crush, and act naturally!

Try not to chase after them at school, particularly assuming they are spending time with their companions and they would appear to prefer not to converse with you. It causes you to appear to be irritating and potentially dreadful

www.ingramcontent.com/pod-product-compliance
Lightning Source LLC
LaVergne TN
LVHW020547160826
845677LV00015B/4240
9798847520683